Messiaen's Musical Language
on the Holy Child

Messiaen's Musical Language on the Holy Child

A Study of *Vingt Regards sur l'Enfant-Jésus, No: XIX: Je dors, mais mon cœur veille, No: XIV: Regard des Anges*

Cagdas Soylar

WIPF & STOCK · Eugene, Oregon

MESSIAEN'S MUSICAL LANGUAGE ON THE HOLY CHILD
A Study of Vingt Regards sur l'Enfant-Jésus, No: XIX: Je dors, mais mon cœur veille, No: XIV: Regard des Anges

Wipf & Stock
An Imprint of Wipf and Stock Publishers
199 W. 8th Ave., Suite 3
Eugene, OR 97401

www.wipfandstock.com

PAPERBACK ISBN: 978-1-5326-6416-8
HARDCOVER ISBN: 978-1-5326-6417-5
EBOOK ISBN: 978-1-5326-6418-2

Manufactured in the U.S.A.   12/05/18

Dedicated to my father and to my mother . . .

A great love is a reflection, a pale reflection, but nevertheless a reflection of the one true love, the divine love.

—OLIVIER MESSIAEN

Contents

List of Figures

Acknowledgements

I WOULD LIKE TO express my deepest appreciation to my supervisor Dr. Paolo Susanni for his guidance, patience and support during this study. I would also like to thank my family and all my friends both in Turkey and in the U.S. for their support and encouragement.

List of Abbreviations

ex.: Example

f: Forte (Loud)

m.: Measure

mf: Mezzo-forte (Moderately loud)

M3: Major-third

m3: Minor-third

No.: Number

pp: Pianissimo (Very soft)

ppp: Pianississimo (As softly as possible)

ST: Semi-tone

T: Tone

Vol.: Volume

Introduction

OLIVIER MESSIAEN WAS A prominent twentieth-century French composer whose works are widely researched and frequently performed. His unique musical language includes highly complicated concepts that are derived from a variety of sources. Greek rhythms, Hindu rhythms, and bird calls influenced him deeply; his Catholic faith, however, had the greatest impact on his compositions. As Messiaen explains in his own words:

> I have been asked to deliver to confession of my faith, that is, to talk about what I believe, what I love, what I hope for. What do I believe? That does not take long to say and in it everything is said at once: I believe in God. And because I believe in God, I believe likewise in the Holy Trinity and especially in the Holy Spirit.[1]

This book gives a detailed analysis of two religiously motivated pieces from the *Vingt Regards Sur l'Enfant-Jésus* (Twenty Gazes upon the Infant Jesus), one of the most remarkable solo piano works of the twentieth-century, to explore how Messiaen integrates Christian theology into his musical language.

Je dors, mais mon cœur veille (I sleep but my heart waketh) is a dialogue that represents Messiaen's mystic love of God, while *Regard des Anges* (Gaze of the Angels) is a celebration that represents the angels beholding the birth of Jesus Christ. Both pieces present diverse pitch collections, musical textures, and rhythmic structures. Different pitch collections have a symbolic meaning for Messiaen. This study examines how the entirely different subjects of the two pieces are articulated in the change of pitch collections

---

1. Kavanaugh, *Spiritual Lives*, 201.

and rhythmic structures. It also shows how the changes of musical language through the use of the different pitch collections generate the formal structure that is related to the biblical source.

As one of the most influential teachers of the twentieth century, Messiaen provided many materials—such as books, programme notes, and interviews—to help future generations understand his compositional technique. These sources are of tremendous help in understanding his religious ideology, his musical language, and the performance of his music.

1.

General Biographical Description

Messiaen's Life

OLIVIER MESSIAEN, FRENCH COMPOSER, organist, ornithologist, and teacher, was born on December 10th, 1908, in Avignon, and died on April 27th, 1992, in Paris. A child prodigy, Messiaen began composing at the age of eight. He studied the piano during his childhood with Gontran Arcouët and Robert Lortart, and studied harmony with Jehan de Gibon.[1] In 1919, he enrolled in the Paris Conservatory where he studied the organ with Marcel Dupré, one of the greatest organists of all time.[2] He left the conservatory in 1931, however, and started working as an organist in the Church of *La Sainte Trinité*, where he held that position until his death. Messiaen also taught at the *École Normale de Musique* and at the *Schola Cantorum*.

At the outbreak of World War II, Messiaen enlisted in the army. Shortly after, he was taken prisoner by the Germans at Görlitz in Silesia and spent the following years (1940–1941) in a prisoner of war camp. Here, he composed his major work, *Quatuor Pour la fin du Temps* (Quartet for the End of Time). The work was composed for himself, to perform at the piano, and a

1. Griffits, *Olivier Messiaen*, 21–23.
2. Griffits, *Olivier Messiaen*, 26.

violinist, a cellist, and a clarinetist, who were also prisoners. They performed their first concert at the camp in the winter of 1941.[3] In the same year, Messiaen was released from the camp. After the war, he started teaching harmony at the Paris Conservatory. Pierre Boulez, Karlheinz Stockhausen, and George Benjamin were his most notable students. In 1966, he became professor of harmony at the Paris Conservatory and retained the position until his retirement in 1978. He died in his sleep on April 27th, 1992, in Paris, at the age of 83.

Messiaen's Catholic faith had the greatest influence on his musical achievements. He devoted himself almost exclusively to his religion, frequently using biblical symbols in his compositions to express his love to Jesus Christ.

Messiaen was also an ornithologist, spending a lot of his time in France and abroad transcribing different bird calls. This was an instinctive passion of his which he did for his own personal joy. He put both the rhythm and melody of bird calls in writing. In France, he could recognize fifty species by their songs; throughout Europe, he could recognize over five hundred others. He composed three masterpieces: *Oiseaux Exotiques* (1955–56) for winds and percussion, *Catalogue d'Oiseaux* (1956–57) for solo piano, and *Chronochromie* (1959–60) for large orchestra. In all of these, Messiaen uses bird calls as melodic material and a kind of musical representation for the holiness of nature. As he explains in his own words, "Among the artistic hierarchy, the birds are probably the greatest musicians to inhabit our planet."[4]

Background of the *Vingt Regards Sur l'Enfant-Jésus*

The *Vingt Regards sur l'Enfant-Jésus* (Twenty Gazes upon the Infant Jesus), composed in 1944, is a masterpiece. The cycle is a good example of his devotion to the Catholic faith as it contains

---

3. Griffits, *Olivier Messiaen*, 90.
4. Johnson, *Messiaen*, 116.

many theological elements and is also considered one of the most remarkable solo piano works of the twentieth-century.

The *Vingt Regards*, as an opus, is subdivided into four groups of five pieces. Every fifth piece addresses the Divinity. The first movement addresses God, the Father, while the fifth addresses God, the Son, and the tenth addresses God, the Holy Spirit. The fifteenth and twentieth movements both address God, the Son.

Messiaen uses three cyclical themes throughout the work. They are the "Theme of God," the "Theme of the Star and the Cross," and the "Theme of Chords." The most important theme is the "God Theme," first heard in the initial movement, *"Regard du Père"* (Gaze of the Father), as it makes up the entire movement. In the first Regard, the theme, which consists of a chordal progression, is in the lower register of the piano, at a pianissimo level. It also occurs in the fifth movement, *"Regard du Fils sur le Fils"* (Gaze of the Son upon the Son) and in the last movement, *"Regard de l'Église d'amour"* (Gaze of the Church of Love). The theme appears again, in incomplete forms, in movements six, ten, eleven and fifteen.

Figure 1. *Thème de Dieu*

1947 by Durand S.A. Editions Musicales, Paris

The *Thème de Dieu*, as a principle theme, includes three secondary themes that appear throughout the composition:

Figure 2. *Thème d'amour*: It appears in four pieces and has different forms. From *Regard de l'Église d'amour* (**No: 20**) (**mm. 31–32**).

1947 by Durand S.A. Editions Musicales, Paris

Figure 3. From *Je dors, mais mon cœur veille* (**No: 19**) (**mm. 24–25**).

1947 by Durand S.A. Editions Musicales, Paris

Figure 4. *Thème du baiser*: It appears in *Le baiser de l'Enfant-Jésus* (**No: 15**) (**mm. 93–94**).

1947 by Durand S.A. Editions Musicales, Paris

Figure 5. *Thème de Joie:* This theme is used in *Regard de l'Esprit de joie* (No: 10) (m. 34).

1947 by Durand S.A. Editions Musicales, Paris

The second theme, the "Theme of the Star and the Cross," is presented in the second movement, *Regard de l'étoile* (Gaze of the Star), and the seventh movement, *Regard de la Croix* (Gaze of the Cross). This is a slow theme, and it consists of small range of intervals representing two significant events in the life of Christ. The first is the lighting of the way for the Magi to find the infant Jesus, while the second represents the crucifixion.

Figure 6. *Thème de l'étoile et de la Croix*

1947 by Durand S.A. Editions Musicales, Paris

Thème de l'étoile et de la Croix includes two motifs that appear throughout the entire work:

Figure 7. *Style Oiseau:* This motif, a birdsong, is used extensively in *Regard des hauteurs* **(No: 8) (mm. 9–13)** and appears most noticeably in the fifth and eighth movements, where the birds sing at the upper range of the piano.

1947 by Durand S.A. Editions Musicales, Paris

Figure 8. *Noël Motif:* Noël motif is a three-note melodic motif that descends by whole-tones and appears in *Noël* **(No: 13) (mm. 5–6).**

1947 by Durand S.A. Editions Musicales, Paris

The third theme, the "Theme of Chords," a four-chord progression, first appears in the sixth movement, *Par Lui tout a été fait* (Through Him everything was made). This theme does not contain any religious references. It also appears in movements six, fourteen, fifteen, sixteen, seventeen, eighteen, and twenty.

Figure 9. *Thème d'accords*

1947 by Durand S.A. Editions Musicales, Paris

Many Biblical references are made in the music, in the movement titles, and in the pre-movement descriptions. The description of the first movement, *Regard du Père* (The gaze of the Father), comes from the New Testament, "This is My beloved Son, in whom I am well-pleased" (Matt 3:17).[5] This pronouncement comes directly after the events described in the previous verse, which states, "After being baptized, Jesus came up immediately from the water; and behold, the heavens were opened, and he saw the Spirit of God descending as a dove and lighting on Him" (Matt 3:16).

Movement six, *Par Lui tout a été fait* (Through Him everything was made), refers to John 1:1–3, with the third verse as its primary source: "In the beginning was the Word, and the Word was with God, and the Word was God. He was in the beginning with God. All things came into being through him, and without him not one thing came into being."[6]

Movement eight, *Regard des hauteurs* (Gaze of the heights), comes from the Christmas story and Luke: "Glory to God in the highest heaven, and on earth peace among those whom he favors!" (Luke 2:14).

The tenth movement, *Regard de l'Esprit de joie* (Gaze of the joyful Spirit) comes from Romans: "For the kingdom of God is not eating and drinking, but righteousness and peace and joy in the Holy Spirit" (Rom 14:17).

The title of the movement twelve, *La parole toute puissante* (The all-powerful word) refers to Hebrews: "The Son is the

5. Burger, "Olivier Messiaen's Vingt Regards," 47.

6. Burger, "Olivier Messiaen's Vingt Regards," 47.

7

radiance of God's glory and the exact representation of his being, sustaining all things by his powerful word" (Heb 1:3).[7] Movement fifteen, *Le baiser de l'Enfant-Jésus* (The kiss of the Infant Jesus), references Revelation: "And God shall wipe away all tears from their eyes; and there shall be no more death, neither sorrow, nor crying, neither shall there be any more pain: for the former things are passed away" (Rev 21:4).

The title of movement nineteen, *Je dors, mais mon cœur veille* (I sleep, but my heart waketh), comes from the Song of Solomon: "I was asleep but my heart was awake. A voice! My beloved was knocking: Open to me, my sister, my darling, My dove, my perfect one! For my head is drenched with dew, My locks with the damp of the night" (Song 5:2).[8]

Biblical numerology seems to play a symbolic role in the *Vingt Regards*. There are several examples of this relationship in the work. For example, movement one, *Regard du Père*, is related to the number one, which is "the number of unity" and evidently represents God, the Father:

> Before me there was no God formed
> Neither shall be or after Me
> I, even, am the Lord
> And besides Me, there is no Saviour. (Isa 43:10–11)[9]

> Hear, O Israel: The Lord our God, the Lord is One. (Deut 6:4)

The multiple of two is also a significant factor, particularly in the numbering of movements six and twelve. In the *Vingt Regards*, this multiple creates a relationship between the two, as both movements deal with the concept of creation, and creation was completed in six days.

Movement seven is dedicated to the Cross because the number seven represents spiritual perfection.[10] As Jesus Christ

---

7. Burger, "Olivier Messiaen's *Vingt Regards*," 47.

8. Burger, "Olivier Messiaen's *Vingt Regards*," 47.

9. Bullinger, *Number in Scripture*, 51.

10. Bullinger, *Number in Scripture*, 23.

sacrificed himself to take away the sins of the world and redeem humanity, movement seven is connected to the spiritual perfection which was provided by Jesus Christ through Cross.

The Title Descriptions of the *Vingt Regards Sur l'Enfant-Jésus*

Messiaen provides title descriptions for each of the *Vingt Regards*. The comments shown below are excerpted from the score, translated by Dennis Vannier.[11] They appear in the following order:

I. Regard du Père (Gaze of the Father)

Complete phrase on the Theme of God.

And God said: "This is my beloved Son, in whom I am well pleased."

II. Regard de l'étoile (Gaze of the star)

Theme of the star and the Cross.

Jolt of grace . . . The star shines naïvely, surmounted by a cross.

III. L'échange (The exchange)

Descent in a trail of light, ascent in a spiral; awesome human-divine communion; God becomes man so that we may become gods.

God is the motif of alternating thirds: that which does not change, that which is small. Man is the remaining fragments, which grow and grow and become huge, following a process of development I call "asymmetrical swelling."

IV. Regard de la Vierge (Gaze of the Blessed Virgin)

Innocence and tenderness . . . The woman of Purity, the woman of the Magnificat, the Blessed Virgin contemplates her Child.

---

11. Voglar, "Fear No Music."

I have tried to express purity in music: this requires a certain degree of strength—coupled with much naïveté and childlike gentleness.

V. Regard du Fils sur le Fils (Gaze of the Son upon the Son)

Mystery, rays of light through the night—refraction of joy, the birds of silence—the person of the Word in a human nature—marriage of the human and divine natures of Jesus Christ.

This represents, of course, the Son-Word contemplating the Son-Child-Jesus. Three sonorities, three modes, three rhythms, three superimposed tunes. "Theme of God" and rhythmic canon through the addition of a dotted note. Joy is represented by birdsongs.

VI. Par Lui tout a été fait (Through Him everything was made)

Multiplicity of spaces and times; galaxies, photons, reverse spirals, inverted thunderbolts; through "Him" (the Word) everything was made . . . in an instant, creation reveals the luminous shadow of its Word.

This is a figure in which the subject is never repeated: as early as the second entrance, it changes rhythm and register. Notice the divertimento during which the upper voice expresses the subject as a non-retrograde rhythm, and where the fortissimo bass repeats a fragment of that subject in asymmetrical swellings. The middle incorporates very short and very long values (representing the infinitely small and infinitely large). Then, retrograde reprise of the fugue, like a crayfish. Mysterious stretta. Fortissimo theme of God: victorious presence, the face of God behind the flames and turmoil. Creation reprises and sings the theme of God as a chordal canon.

VII. Regard de la Croix (Gaze of the Cross)

Theme of the star and the Cross.

The Cross said to him: you shall be priest in my arms.

VIII. Regard des hauteurs (Gaze of the heights)

Glory in the heights . . . the heights descend upon the manger like the song of a lark . . . Birdsongs: nightingales, thrushes, warblers, chaffinches, goldfinches, warblers, serins, and mostly larks.

IX. Regard du Temps (Gaze of time)

Mystery of the plenitude of time; Time sees within itself the birth of He who is eternal.

This theme is short, cold, strange, like de Chirico's egglike heads; rhythmic canon.

X. Regard de l'Esprit de joie (Gaze of the Spirit of joy)

Vehement dance, drunken horn-like tonalities, transport of the Holy Spirit . . . the joy of God's love in the soul of Jesus Christ.

I have always been struck by the fact that God is happy—and that His continual and ineffable joy inhabited the soul of Christ. Joy is, for me, a transport, an intoxication in the maddest sense.

Form:

Oriental dance in the extreme-low range, in unequal neumes, like plainchant. First development on the "theme of joy." Asymmetrical swelling. Three hunting-tune-like variations. Second development on the "theme of joy" and "theme of God." Then, reprise of the Oriental dance, with the extreme-low and extreme-high ranges together. Coda on the "theme of joy."

XI. Première communion de la Vierge (First communion of the Blessed Virgin)

A tableau in which the Blessed Virgin is shown kneeling, bent forward in the night—a luminous halo surrounds her form. Her eyes shut, she worships the fruit hidden within herself. This scene takes place between the Annunciation and the Nativity: it is the first and greatest of communions.

Theme of God, soft volutes, stalactites, and interior embrace. Recall of the theme of the "Virgin and Child" in my "Nativity."

Ever more enthusiastic Magnificat. Special chords with pulsations in the low register, representing the heart of the beating Child within his mother's breast. The theme of God vanishes.

After the Annunciation, the Virgin Mary worships Jesus within herself . . . my God, my Son, my Magnificat!—my love without voice.

XII. La parole toute puissante (The all-powerful Word)

Monody with pulsations in the low register.

This child is the Word, which sustains all things though the power of its voice.

XIII. Noël (Christmas)

Carillon—the bells of Christmas sing with us the sweet names of Jesus, Mary, Joseph.

XIV. Regard des Anges (Gaze of the Angels)

Shimmering, percussion; powerful breaths sounding immense trombones; thy servants are flames of fire . . . and then, the songs of birds drinking azure—and the angels are amazed: for God has joined, not with them, but with the human race . . .

In the first three stanzas: flames, rhythmic canon, and breaking up of the chordal theme.

Fourth stanza: birdsongs. Fifth stanza: the angels are amazed.

XV. Le baiser de l'Enfant Jésus (The kiss of the Child Jesus)

At every communion, the Child Jesus sleeps beside us near the door; He then opens it upon a garden and throws Himself in the light to embrace us.

Theme of God in the style of a lullaby. Sleep—the garden—arms extended toward love—the kiss—the shadow of the kiss. An etching furnished my inspiration for this movement: it showed the Child Jesus leaving the arms of His mother to kiss little sister Thérèse. All this is symbolic of communion, of divine love. One must love in order to love that picture and this music, which aims to be as soft as the heart of heaven; there is nothing else.

XVI. Regard des prophètes, des bergers et des Mages (Gaze of the prophets, the shepherds, and the magi)

Exotic music—tom-toms and hautboys, huge and reedy consort.

XVII. Regard du silence (Gaze of silence)

Silence in the palm of the hand, inverted rainbow . . . Every silence in the manger reveals music and color that are the mysteries of Jesus Christ.

Polymodality, rhythmic canon through the addition of a dotted note, special chords, "theme of chords." The entire piece is intricately chiseled, for a piano work. Ending: alternating chords, multicolored and impalpable music, like confetti, light gemstones, and colliding reflections.

XVIII. Regard de l'Onction terrible (Gaze of the awesome anointing)

The Word assumes its human nature; awesome Majesty adopts Jesus's flesh.

An ancient tapestry depicts the Word of God as combat, with Christ astride a charger: one sees only His two hands clasping the hilt of a sword, which He brandishes through a cloud of lightning bolts. That image influenced me. In the introduction and the coda, gradually slowing notes are superimposed on gradually accelerating notes, and vice versa.

XIX. Je dors, mais mon cœur veille (I sleep, but my heart waketh)

Love poem, dialogue of mystical love. Rests play an important part.

It is not the angel's bow that smiles down on us—it is sleeping Jesus, who loves us on His Sunday and grants us oblivion.

XX. Regard de l'Eglise d'amour (Gaze of the Church of love)

Grace makes us love God as He loves Himself; after the rays of night and the spirals of distress, here are the bells, the glory, and the loving kiss ... The full passion of our arms embracing the Invisible.

Form (the development precedes the exposition):

Development:

First theme in a non-retrograde rhythm, amplified to the right and left; that theme is interrupted by inverted fireworks. Then, three recalls of the "theme of God" separated by asymmetrical swellings. The third theme is melodic. It is followed by the first theme with fireworks and more asymmetrical swelling. Finally, ringing of bells, forming a dominant pedal and recalling the chords of the preceding movements.

Exposition:

Complete phrase on the "theme of God," as a glorious fanfare. Long coda on the "theme of God"—triumph of love and joy, tears of joy.

2.

Messiaen's Source of Materials

Modes of Limited Transposition

The most important feature of Messiaen's compositional technique is a group of modes known as the modes of limited transposition. These constitute a system of seven symmetrical modes which have a limited number of transpositions before they replicate themselves. In other words, a mode can only be transposed a limited number of times before replicating itself in its original state. As Messiaen describes in his own words:

> Based on our chromatic system, a tempered system of twelve-sounds, these modes are formed of several symmetrical groups, the last of each group always being common with the first of the following group. At the end of a certain number of chromatic transpositions, which varies with each mode, they are no longer transposable, the fourth transposition giving exactly the same notes as the first, for example, the fifth giving exactly the same notes as the second, etc.[1]

The first mode is the whole-tone scale, which consists exclusively of whole-tones. This mode has two possible transpositions.[2]

1. Messiaen, *Technique*, 58.
2. There are only two whole-tone scales: the WT 0 (C-D-E-F♯-G♯-A♯-C),

The second mode is the octatonic scale. This scale is an eight-note scale arranged in alternating tone and semitones.[3] It has only three possible transpositions.

Figure 10. Mode 2, *Technique of My Musical Language,* **vol. 2, ex. 316.**

The third mode is structured according to a T-ST-ST sequence and has four possible transpositions.

Figure 11. Mode 3, *Technique of My Musical Language,* **vol. 2, ex. 329.**

The fourth mode interval sequence is ST-ST-m3-ST and has six possible transpositions.

Figure 12. Mode 4, *Technique of My Musical Language,* **vol. 2, ex. 345.**

The fifth mode is structured according to the ST-M3-ST interval pattern and has six possible transpositions.

Figure 13. Mode 5, *Technique of My Musical Language,* **vol. 2, ex. 347.**

Mode 6 consists of two overlapping pentachords, each consisting of two consecutive whole-tones followed by two consecutive semitones.

---

and the WT 1 (C♯-D♯-F-G-A-B-C♯).

3. The three standard models of the octatonic scale are based on the tone-semitone pattern and are therefore the following: Octatonic-0 (C-D-E♭-F-F♯-G♯-A-B-C), Octatonic-1 (C♯-D♯-E-F♯-G-A-B♭-C-C♯), and Octatonic-2 (D-E-F-G-A♭-B♭-B-C♯-D).

Figure 14. Mode 6, *Technique of My Musical Language,* **vol. 2, ex. 350.**

Mode 7 is generated by an ST-ST-ST-T-ST-ST-ST-ST-T-ST interval pattern and has six possible transpositions.

Figure 15. Mode 7, *Technique of My Musical Language,* **vol. 2, ex. 354.**

Rhythmic Structures

Rhythms with Added Values

Rhythm is arguably the most difficult feature of Messiaen's music to understand. His interest in a wide array of asymmetrical rhythms is a fundamental part of his music. Most often, highly complex and varying rhythms have no time signatures. Although the rhythms are associated with regular meters, they have irregularly added and deleted values.

An added value is a short value that can be added to any rhythm in the form of either notes, rests, or dots.[4] This kind of addition to a rhythm makes the rhythm's value irregular and flexible.

Figure 16. Added value

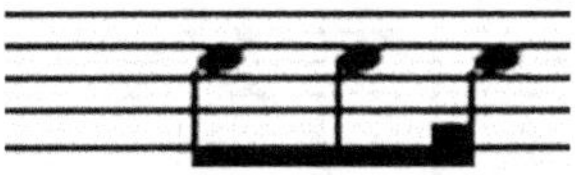

Augmented and Diminished Rhythms

One of the fundamental aspects of Messiaen's music is the technique of augmentation and diminution of a given rhythm. He frequently uses a rhythm followed by its immediate augmentation or diminution.

4. Messiaen, *Technique,* 16.

Figure 17. *Technique of My Musical Language,* **vol. 2, ex. 20.**

He applies this technique in one of two ways: exactly (in a systematic manner) or inexactly (in an irregular manner).

Example of an inexact augmentation:

Figure 18. *Technique of My Musical Language,* **vol. 2, ex. 25.**

Table of Augmentation

Figure 19. *Technique of My Musical Language,* **vol. 2, ex. 24.**

Augmentation of the quarter of the values	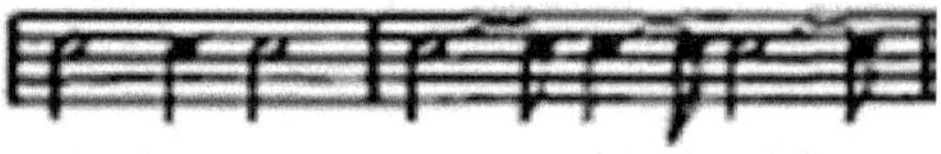
Augmentation of a third of the values	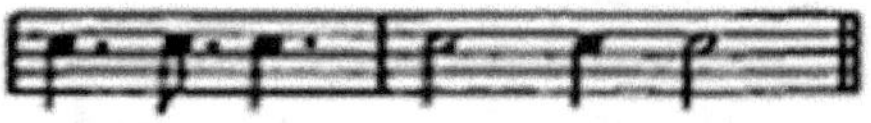
Augmentation of the dot (half of the values)	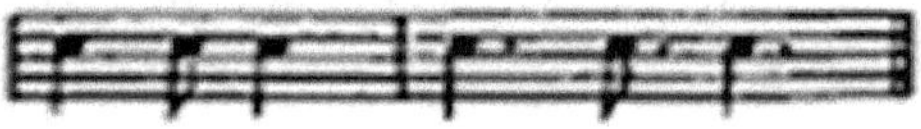
Classic augmentation (augmentation of the values to themselves)	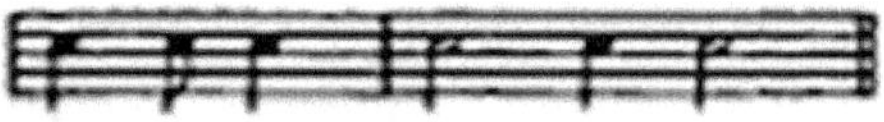
Augmentation of two times of the values	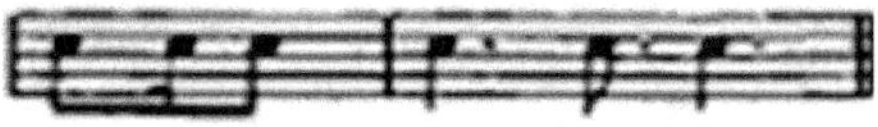
Augmentation of three times of the vaues	
Augmentation of four times of the values	

Table of Diminution

Figure 20. *Technique of My Musical Language,* **vol. 2, ex. 24.**

Diminution of a fifth of the values	
Diminution of a quarter of the values	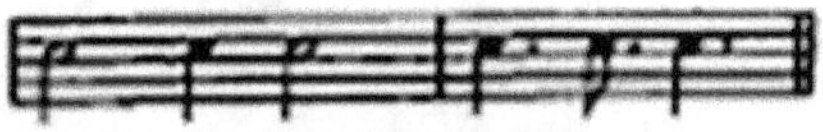
Diminution of the dot (a third of the values)	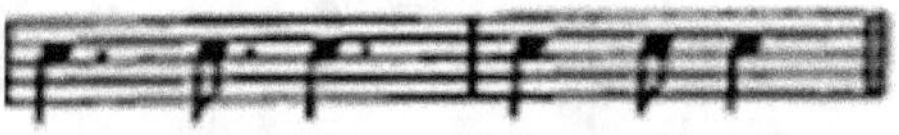
Classic Diminution (half of the values)	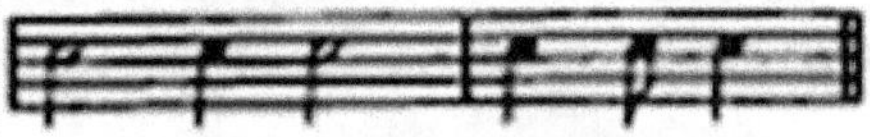
Diminution of the two-thirds of the values	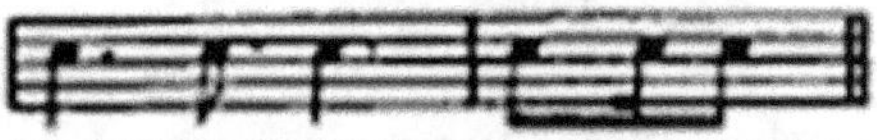
Diminution of three-quarters of the values	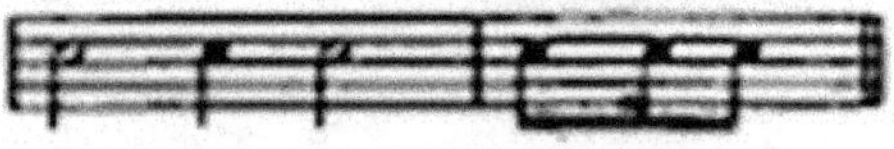
Diminution of four-fifths of the values	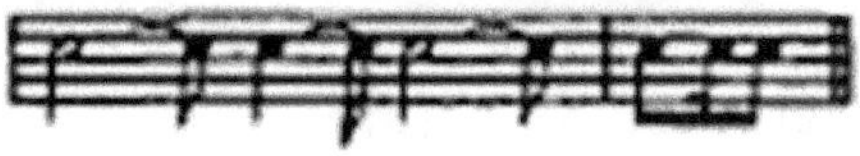

Non-Retrogradable Rhythms

Olivier Messiaen gives a clear explanation of what non-retrogradable rhythms are: "Whether one reads them from right to left or from left to right, the order of their values remains the same."[5] He also indicates that "all rhythms divisible into two groups, one of which is the retrograde of the other, with a central common value, are non-retrogradable."[6] This symmetrical system of rhythmic structuring is one the fundamental features of his compositions. He derived this structure from Hindu rhythms called *deçî-tâlas* and used it frequently.

Figure 21. *Technique of My Musical Language,* **vol. 2, ex. 31.**

5. Messiaen, *Technique,* 20.
6. Messiaen, *Technique,* 20.

Rhythmic Pedals

The simplest explanation of rhythmic pedal is that rhythm which repeats itself, in ostinato. Messiaen describes it as a "rhythm which repeats itself indefatigably, in ostinato . . . without busying itself about the rhythms which surround it."[7]

Figure 22. *Regards du fils sur le fils* (No: 5) (mm. 8–11).

1947 by Durand S.A. Editions Musicales, Paris

Harmonic Structures

The Chord in Fourths

Messiaen uses six-note chords that consist of alternating augmented and perfect fourths. The six-note—or "complete"—version of the chord is often subdivided into smaller, three-note partitions.

Figure 23. *Technique of My Musical Language*, vol. 2, ex. 213.

7. Messiaen, *Technique*, 26.

The Chord on the Dominant

The chord on the dominant includes all the notes of the major scale.[8]

Figure 24. *Technique of My Musical Language,* **vol. 2, ex. 201.**

Below is the primary resolution of the chords on the dominant.

Figure 25. *Technique of My Musical Language,* **vol. 2, ex. 202.**

Generally, two-note appoggiaturas follow this seven-note structure.

Figure 26. *Technique of My Musical Language,* **vol. 2, ex. 203.**

The Chord of Resonance

Messiaen describes the chord of resonance: "Nearly all the notes perceptible, to an extremely fine ear, in the resonance of a low C, figured, tempered, in this chord."[9] They are frequently voiced as a

8. Messiaen, *Technique,* 50.
9. Messiaen, *Technique,* 50.

dominant-seventh chord in the left hand and a half-diminished seventh chord in the right hand. They are often presented in their different inversions.

Figure 27. *Technique of My Musical Language,* **vol. 2, ex. 208.**

Example of the inversions on a common bass note (C-sharp or D-flat).

Figure 28. *Technique of My Musical Language,* **vol. 2, ex. 209.**

All the notes of the third mode of limited transpositions are presented by the chord of the resonance.

Figure 29. *Technique of My Musical Language,* **vol. 2, ex. 211.**

3.

No: XIX Je Dors, Mais Mon Cœur Veille

Love poem, dialogue of mystical love. Rests play an important part.

It is not the angel's bow that smiles down on us

it is sleeping Jesus, who loves us on His Sunday and grants us oblivion.

Musical Language and Rhythmic Structure

JE DORS, MAIS MON *cœur veille* (I sleep, but my heart waketh) comes from the Song of Solomon: "I was asleep but my heart was awake. A voice! My beloved was knocking: Open to me, my sister, my darling, My dove, my perfect one! For my head is drenched with dew, My locks with the damp of the night" (Song 5:2).

Immediately after the main title, the additional title of *Je dors, mais mon cœur veille* starts with a phrase representing Saint Francis of Assisi ("It is not an angel's bow that smiles"). Saint Francis asks God to give him the pleasure of eternal life and then sees an angel holding a violin and a bow in his hands. When the angel starts to play, Francis becomes amazed by the beauty of the melody and loses his sense of physical sensation. He later tells everyone that he got scared of his soul being separated from his body from the intolerable pleasure. At the beginning of the piece, Messiaen promises that the unbearable joy is not coming from the angel's bow: "It is sleeping Jesus who loves us on his Sunday and gives us oblivion."[1]

The slow *Je dors, mais mon cœur veille* is a dialogue that represents Messiaen's mystic love of God and might be divided into three parts related to the musical language, the form, and the title of the piece. The first twenty-three measures form Section A, (mm. 24–68) Section B, and (mm. 69–87) Section A'. The movement is indeed in ternary form, in which all of the sections are made up of smaller portions.

Section A:

The opening section (mm. 1–24) consists of two distinct parts. The first part (mm. 1–8) is diatonic and made up exclusively of an F♯ major triad. The second part (mm. 9–24) is exclusively octatonic.

The F♯ major key signature is confirmed by the unchanging F♯ major 6/3 chord (mm. 1–7). Since there is no harmonic or melodic activity to generate a musical direction or phrase, rests (m. 8) act as a cadence to mark the end of the section.

Figure 30. (mm. 1–8)

1. Bruhn, *Images and Ideas*, 276.

Messiaen appreciated both vertical and horizontal symmetry in music. Having a perfect fourth between two thirds, the F♯ major triad in first inversion with the third doubled is such an example. The F♯ triad is used as a symbol to create God's image in this movement.[2] Therefore, the key signature F♯ most likely represents God, the Son. As there is no conclusive cadence at the end of the opening section (mm. 8–9), the key signature of the piece is definitely meant to be used as a symbol. The F♯ major scale has six accidentals: F♯-C♯-G♯-D♯-A♯-E♯. Messiaen stated that the number six is a symbol for the creation of humankind, which was completed in six days—as mentioned in the book of Genesis.[3] This six-sharp key signature and its six-part harmony are related to creation as mentioned in the Bible and are not a true statement of tonality.

The relationship between time and eternity is also one of the fundamental conceptions of Messiaen's musical output. The lack of a time signature suggests that time is uninterrupted. It also emphasizes God's eternity, as God does not have a beginning or an end.[4]

This section is associated with the title of the movement as well as the first stanza of the Song of Solomon 5:2 "I was asleep but my heart was awake." It undoubtedly represents the sleeping Jesus (mm. 1–7). The *pp* at the beginning of the piece plays an important part in creating quietness. The rhythmic variations of the first measure (mm. 3–6) describe how Jesus keeps watching us, even when he is sleeping.

Every added value that occurs in the opening section (mm. 1–8) is on the chord of F♯ 6/3. As the added value is a new duration of the given rhythm, the use of this added value creates asymmetry in the texture. In the initial eight-note rhythm, the added value (m. 3) is represented by a sixteenth-note. The first three eighth notes are represented in six sixteenth-notes and are immediately

2. Bruhn, *Messiaen's Contemplations*, 47.

3. Bruhn, *Messiaen's Explorations*, 221.

4. Bruhn, *Messiaen's Language*, 37.

followed by an eighth-note. It is precisely the sixteenth-note that creates an asymmetrical growth in the text.

Figure 31. (m. 3)

1947 by Durand S.A. Editions Musicales, Paris

Messiaen truly appreciated rhythmic freedom. He admired those small entities of music that destroy the systematic subdivision of metric units. He added a sixteenth-note to one of the values in almost every measure of the opening section in order to ruin human notions of time.

There is a sudden change of musical texture at a *mf* dynamic level (m. 9). Mode 2 or the octatonic 1 scale emerges as the primary pitch collection not only of this formal section but also of the entire piece.

Figure 32. (mm. 9–17)

In terms of scales, there is no logical musical connection between the opening section and m. 9. The new part of the large A is suddenly separated from the opening. It is very unusual, however, to go from one part to another without a development. As Messiaen did not compose either in the traditional tonal system or in the atonal system, these hints given by the formal structure would be the only way to understand how the musical development is directly connected to the title. For instance, the new dynamic mark is *mf* followed by *f* (m. 11). This dynamic change right on the octatonic scale might suggest that the new section no longer represents the sleeping Jesus. The second part is related to the composer's description: "The dialogue of mystical love." Mode 2 is distributed in right-hand/left-hand alternations (m. 9, 11, 15, and 17) to literally represent the dialogue.

It is interesting to note that the main beats of the left hand of the octatonic section (m. 9) are perfect fourths [C♯-F♯, A♯-D♯ and

G-B♯(C)]. In the next measure (m. 10), the main beats of the left hand are also made up of the perfect fourth [E-A] and its inversion, the perfect fifth [A-E]. The F♯ minor seventh chord (m. 10) is, according to Messiaen, related to the octatonic scale because F♯ minor seventh chord can be derived from octatonic 1. As the F♯ minor seventh chord does not include an A♯, the new part of the large A is still not related to the opening, which is entirely made of an F♯ major chord. The chords of the right hand (m. 12) are also made up of perfect fifths [F♯-C♯-G♯-D♯]. All of these perfect fourths and fifths are abstracted from the diatonic aspect of the octatonic scale. The chords of m. 10 and m. 14 create an identical pattern with the appearance of the D♯ minor seventh chord (m. 14). Therefore, the diatonic aspect of the first part of the opening section is used again. This relation also suggests that the composer wants to give an impression of returning the God theme at a *pp* dynamic level although this would not be a real return. There is indeed a clash between the diatonic scale and the octatonic scale (mm. 9–14). The clash between the diatonic and octatonic scale comes to an end (m. 16) in much the same way as a cadence that marks the end of a tonal phrase. In addition, the texture is immediately changed in the subsequent measure (m. 17).

The complete pitch content of (mm. 17–22) is octatonic. The reappearance of the D♯ minor seventh chord (m. 22) proves that whenever the octatonic content is used, it is resolved by a diatonic content. Even though these two parts of the A section use a very different pitch context, strong links that are common to both are used to link them.

There are approximately three-hundred verses that talk about birds in the Bible. They sometimes appear as the symbol of purity, or are given a spiritual meaning. Proverbs says, "As a bird that wandereth from her nest, so is a man that wandereth from his place" (Prov 27:8). Messiaen was deeply interested in bird songs and frequently used them in his compositions to explain his love of nature being closely related to God. He admired the idea of "exemplarism," developed by Bonaventure, one of the Franciscan theologians of the thirteenth-century. Exemplarism means that one can recognize God through the creatures around him as these creatures in nature reflect their Creator.[5] He uses a small bird motif on the second beat of (m. 12) in an incomplete chromatic scale as an introduction to its frequent appearance in the large B section. The birds always appear in a chromatic scale in the upper range of the piano.

The special treatment of rhythm is an essential part of Messiaen's music and sometimes suggests the birth of time mentioned in the Bible. Messiaen writes:

> Let us not forget that the first, essential element in music is Rhythm, and that Rhythm is, first and foremost, the change of number and duration. Suppose that there were a single beat in all the universe. One beat; with eternity before it and eternity after it. A before and an after. That is the birth of time. Imagine then, almost immediately, a second beat. Since any beat is prolonged by the silence which follows it, the second beat will be longer than the first. Another number, another duration. That is the birth of Rhythm.[6]

A sixteenth note is placed on the downbeat of the measure (m. 18) so that the shorter note at the beginning of the measure causes an ametrical rhythmic flow and most probably suggests the birth of time as a singularity, as happens in the book of Genesis.

Figure 33. (m. 18)

1947 by Durand S.A. Editions Musicales, Paris

5. Bruhn, *Messiaen's Contemplations*, 65.

6. Bruhn, *Messiaen's Language*, 47.

The rests at the end of the second section (m. 23) again act as a cadence to mark its end.

Figure 34. (mm. 21–23)

1947 by Durand S.A. Editions Musicales, Paris

The *Thème d'amour*—a subsidiary theme to the *Thème de Dieu*—is introduced at the beginning of section B (m. 24) at a *forte* dynamic level. This sudden dynamic change represents the imploring nature of the words in the Song of Solomon, "A voice! My beloved was knocking: Open to me, my sister, my darling, My dove, my perfect one! For my head is drenched with dew, My locks with the damp of the night" (Song 5:2). *Thème d'amour* is presented with an incomplete E♭ minor chord in the right hand the first time it appears. This unexpected representation of the theme is accompanied by whole-tone chords of the left hand.

Section B:

Figure 35. (mm. 24–30)

1947 by Durand S.A. Editions Musicales, Paris

The third chord of the left hand (m. 24) is an incomplete whole-tone 0 collection [A♭-B♭-C-D]. The second chord is an incomplete whole-tone 1 [A-B-C♯-D♯]. The chord of the first triplet [C-E-G-A] is made up of both whole-tone scale fragments where [C-E] belongs to whole-tone 0 and [G-A] belongs to whole-tone 1. As a result, the first triplet represents both whole-tone scales which are separated out in the next two chords. It is interesting to note that whole-tone scales are used to represent the "Theme of Love" which appears right at the beginning of Section B (m. 24). Because the whole-tone scale does not contain any semi-tones—which can be heard as leading tones—and therefore creates harmonic tension, it is perhaps one of the best pitch collections to represent the "Theme of Love" and especially apt to represent the human love of God.

The left hand of (m. 25) consists of alternations of octatonic chords. The notes of the left hand chords are the octatonic 1 collection [C♯-E-G-A] and the octatonic 0 collection [C-E♭-G♭-A♭]. Opposed to these is the perfect fourth interval of the right hand [E♭-B♭], which, once again, represents the clash between diatonic and octatonic realms. The chords that immediately follow (m. 26) are also alternations of the octatonic collections. The first [G-D-B-F-B♭] is octatonic 2, the second [E♭-B♭-G-D♭-G♭] is octatonic 1, while the third [F-C-A-E♭-F] is octatonic 0. Simultaneously, six notes of the perfect fifth cycle [E♭-B♭-F-C-G-D] are present in the lower part, manifesting the ongoing clash between the two different collections. To cement the octatonic aspect, the chords of the left hand (m. 27) are all octatonic fragments, [C-F♯-A-D] being octatonic 0, [G-C] being octatonic 1, and [G♯-B] being octatonic 2. With the exception of A, the last chord [B-D-E-G♯-A] represents octatonic 2.

While mode 6 suddenly appears for the first time at the tempo change, (m. 28) represented by block chords in both hands, mode 2, the primary pitch collection of the entire piece, emerges in the subsequent measure [C♯-D-E-F-G-A♭-A♯-B].

Immediately after this (m. 30), octatonic combinations recommence. The first chord and the second chord are octatonic 1

[C-D♯-F♯-(G♯)-A♯ and C-E-F♯-A-E], while the third and fourth chords are octatonic 0 [A-D♯-F♯-B-F and F♯-C-F-(A♯)-B]. The fifth chord consists of a diatonic collection [F-B-E-A-D] which is in cyclic order. The final chord is exclusively octatonic [D♯-F♯-B-E-A♯]. The left hand of the entire measure consists of tritons, where half of the octatonic 1 scale can be derived from the first four sixteenth-notes. The octatonic 0 collection [G♯-F♯-E♯-B-D] is unfolded horizontally by the top notes. This octatonism is brought to a sudden end by the chords of the following measure (m. 31).

The first chord [G♯-A♯-C𝄪-E♯] is an incomplete whole-tone collection, while the second chord [E-B-A-D-F♯-G♯-A♯(B♭)-F] is an incomplete perfect fifth cycle, completed by the notes of the next two chords. [B-F♯-C♯-G♯-E♭-B♭-C-G]. The "Theme of Love" appears immediately after. The third repetition of the "Theme of Love" ends (m. 39) with the confirmation of the cyclic aspect, which occurs in the perfect fifths [B-F♯-C♯-G♯].

There is a return to the octatonic aspect shortly after (m. 42) where the first chord is octatonic 2 [B♭-F-D-A♭-C♯], the second chord is octatonic 1 [F♯-C♯-A♯-E-A], and the third chord is octatonic 0 [D♯-F♯-G♯-B♯]. Immediately after that, the whole-tone 1 collection reappears (m. 44) [C♯-D♯-E♯-B] with the exception of A♯. Octatonic 2 follows (m. 45) [C♯-D-E♯-B], with the reappearance of the chords found in the first measure.

Asymmetrical expansion plays an important role in Messiaen's music. The immediate growth of rhythms can also explain Jesus Christ's abundant love. Siglind Bruhn explains that one of the most important themes that can be seen in Messiaen's music is God's Love, and this love is extended to the world through Jesus Christ. For instance, in movement *L'échange*, Messiaen describes God as "that which does not move" with humanity, "represented by fragments that grow and grow and become enormous, in a process that I call 'asymmetric growth.'"[7]

7. Bruhn, *Messiaen's Contemplations*, 159.

Figure 36. (mm. 43–53)

1947 by Durand S.A. Editions Musicales, Paris

Once again, there is a new clash between whole-tone 1 (m. 46) [C♯-D♯-E♯-(A♯)-B] with the octatonic 1 [C♯-D♯-E-F♯-G-A♯] (m. 48) and octatonic 0 collections (m. 49) [F♯-G♯-B-D]. There is a repetition of the section with minor changes. After a repetition of all the presented materials (mm. 50–61), the sudden entrance of the *Thème d'accords* confirms the cyclic aspect (m. 62) by yielding a stream of perfect fourths in the top part [E♯-F♯-G♯-F♯-A♯-B-C♯] that combine with the lower part [B-F♯-C♯-G♯-E♭-B♭-C] to unfold the complete perfect fourth cycle.

A new repetition of the *Thème d'accords* introduces Section B.

Figure 37. (m. 62)

In *Je Dors, Mais Mon Cœur Veille*, the connection of the themes with specific pitch collections remains unchanged, so that their meaning does not change as well. The *Thème d'accords* is in a chromatic scale represented by four successive vertical structures. New bird motifs appear in a chromatic scale on the third beat of (mm. 54–59) and, as before, they are presented at the upper range of the piano. As Messiaen explains: "Melodies of the 'bird' genre will be transcription, transformation, and interpretation of the volleys and trills of our little servants of immaterial joy."[8]

---

8. Messiaen, *Technique of My Musical Language*, 34.

Figure 38. (mm. 54–59)

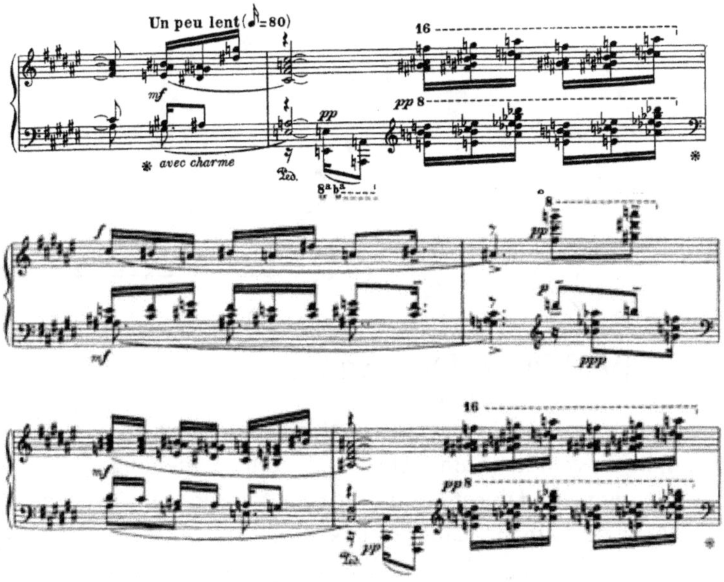

1947 by Durand S.A. Editions Musicales, Paris

Being directly related to the text from the Song of Solomon, "My dove, my perfect one" (Song 6:9), these bird calls definitely stand as reflections of their Creator.

Section A':

Being in ternary form, the return of a modified A section (m. 69) occurs. The F♯ major chord used as the primary chord of the opening returns to open the third section and is followed by a short coda (m. 79), ending the piece at a *ppp* level.

The changes of musical language through the use of the different pitch collections generate the formal structure of the piece. Section A (mm. 1–24) consists of diatonic and octatonic pitch collections. Section B (mm. 24–68) contains whole-tone scales, diatonic and octatonic pitch collections. Section A' (mm. 69–87) is made up of the same diatonic collection as section A.

4.

No: XIV Regard Des Anges

Shimmering, percussion; powerful breaths sounding immense trombones; thy servants are flames of fire . . . and then, the songs of birds drinking azure—and the angels are amazed: for God has joined, not with them, but with the human race . . .

In the first three stanzas: flames, rhythmic canon, and breaking up of the chordal theme.

Fourth stanza: birdsongs. Fifth stanza: the angels are amazed.

Musical Language and Rhythmic Structure

REGARD DES ANGES IS about the decision of God becoming human. It is about the angels beholding the birth of Jesus Christ. The form of the piece can be represented in the following manner: Section A (mm. 1–18), Section A' (mm. 19–43), Section A" (mm. 44–77), Section B (mm. 78–133) and Coda (mm. 134–156).

Section A is joyful in character, represented by flames of fire. The sound of the trombone represents the celebration of Jesus Christ's arrival in human form and includes rhythmic canon and a fragmented chordal theme.

The opening of *Regard des Anges* (mm. 1–4) is derived directly from the second transposition of mode 7 [C#-D-D#-E-F#-G-G#-A-A#-B].

Figure 39. (mm. 1–4)

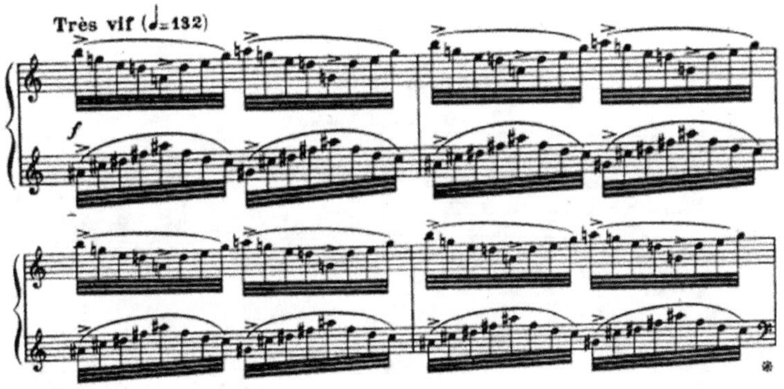

The alternate notes of the complete texture (left-hand and right-hand) outline a nine-note segment of the perfect fifth cycle [G-D-E-A-B-F♯-C♯-G♯-D♯-A♯-C] breaking up mode 7 into its perfect fifth components. This cyclic aspect is confirmed by its transformation into vertical representations in the first and second chords of measure (m. 5) [B♭-E♭/G♯-C♯/G-C/F♯-B] and in the subsequent measure (m. 6) [E-B/D-A/A-E/D-A/C-G/G-D]. In these same measures, the perfect fifth aspect continues to exist in the left hand, however, octatonic pitch collections are also introduced for the first time in the right hand [B-D-F♯-E♯/G♯-B♯-F♯/F♯-A♯-E]. Here, the *Thème d'accords* (mm. 5–6) with its customary added values, unfolds.

Figure 40. (mm. 5–6)

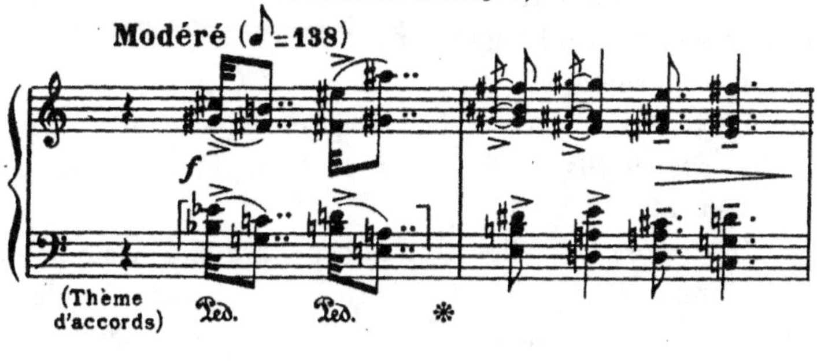

37

The trombones are introduced (m. 9) and follow one another in a strict rhythmic canon.

Figure 41. (mm. 8–17)

1947 by Durand S.A. Editions Musicales, Paris

In this rhythmic canon, one can derive augmented and diminished rhythms, rhythmic pedals, added values and non-retrogradable rhythms. Different sonorities and rhythmic structures are used to introduce new themes or ideas throughout the piece. The added value in the *Thème d'accords*, together with the rhythmic canon of the trombones, are the only two rhythmic devices used to identify the themes themselves.

The octatonic aspect of the passage emerges and is confirmed by the tritones [B♭-E/C♯-G] derived from the octatonic scale (mm. 7–13).

The texture that follows is clearly divided into octatonic and perfect fifth cyclic segments. The left hand consists of two different octatonic collections, (mm. 14–15) is the octatonic 2 collection [B-D-F-E] and (mm. 16–18) is octatonic 0 [A-C-G♯-E♭-B-D]. Above these, the right hand continues to unfold perfect fifths horizontally.

This is followed by the repetition of the first four measures, which forms section A' (mm. 19–22).

Unlike section A, A' is followed by a new motif that explores octatonic, cyclic, and whole-tone formations (mm. 23–24), where [Ab-C-D-Gb] is octatonic 0, [A-E-B] are perfect fifths, [Eb-F-Db-G] is whole-tone 1 and [G-F#-C-A#-E] is octatonic 1. Immediately following this motif, the *Modere* part of Section A is repeated with a small extension (m. 44). A similar thing happens with the repetition of A as A", with increasingly larger extension. These extensions, however, are not significant in presenting new pitch collections (mm. 48–77).

Section B (mm. 78–133) is called "*comme un oiseau*" which means "like a bird." This section is a close imitation of the birds one finds in his bird song collections and contains all the pitch collections used in the first three sections of the piece.

In the Coda (mm. 134–156), the emphasis is purely on the octatonic collections, where all three octatonic scales are represented in alternating measures, for example, (mm. 138–139–140).

Regard des Anges is very different from *Je dors mais mon cœur veille* in terms of form and musical language. *Je dors mais mon cœur veille* starts with a definite mode, whereas *Regard des Anges* begins with pure perfect fifth cycles.

Modes seem to represent the human aspect of existence because they are made up of unequal parts. On the other hand, the cycles, being made up of equal and repeating intervals, seem to represent something quite different. Quite possibly, the universal. In the cases of both pieces, the type of pitch construction the composer uses in different sections symbolizes the ideas put forward in the descriptions at the beginning. They are also in part responsible for the formal definition of the pieces.

Regard des Anges shows various features of his composition style, such as rhythmic augmentations and diminutions, non-retrogradable rhythms, and rhythmic pedals. An example of exact rhythmic augmentation is present in the *Thème d'accords* (m. 6), with the third and fourth chords serving as augmentations of those that came before.

Figure 42. (m. 6)

A non-retrogradable rhythmic structure occurs in Section A' (m. 32), where the rhythmic sequence is palindromic. Messiaen was deeply interested in non-retrogradable rhythms because the music rhythmically returns to its starting point. The use of non-retrogradable rhythms suggests Messiaen's desire to return to God. This motion is directly suggested in the Bible: "And the dust returns to the earth as it was, and the spirit returns to God who gave it" (Eccl 12:7).

Figure 43. (m. 32)

An eighth rest is placed on the downbeat of the measure (m. 23) so that the short rest at the beginning of the measure causes an ametrical rhythmic flow.

Figure 44. (m. 23)

1947 by Durand S.A. Editions Musicales, Paris

In conclusion, the musical language and the use of the different pitch collections act together to generate the formal structure.

Section A (mm. 1–18) consists of perfect fifth cycles and octatonic collections. Section A' (mm. 19–43) consists of cyclic, octatonic, and whole-tone collections. Section A" (mm. 44–77) consists of the same collections found in A'. Section B (mm. 78–133) returns to the cyclic and octatonic collections, the latter of which becomes the exclusive collections of the Coda (mm. 134–156).

5.

Conclusion

Je Dors, Mais Mon Cœur Veille and *Regard des Anges* deal
with two vastly different subjects. These are articulated through
changes of pitch collections and rhythmic structures. For example, as explained in chaper 3, *Je Dors, Mais Mon Cœur Veille*, the
first part of the opening section is made up of the symmetrical
inversion of the F♯ major, which symbolizes God's perfection.
The "Theme of Love" (m. 24) is represented by the whole-tone
scale, which does not contain any semitones, and therefore lacks
harmonic tension. This collection represents the human love of
God. Because of their equal intervals, the perfect fourth and fifth
cycles always represent divine and universal concepts throughout the entire piece. Each theme has its own pitch collections,
and the sequence of the themes helps create the form of the piece.
Messiaen places these themes in different places to create the
progression of musical events encompassed by the title.

In *Regard des Anges*, at the beginning of the first stanza, the
word "shimmering" is given by the first four measures with the
presentation of mode 7. Another universal concept is articulated
by equal intervals, presented through alternating perfect fifths.
Because alternating fifths cannot be derived from the octatonic
sequence, Messiaen uses mode 7, which is not only presented as a
mode but also as a perfect fifth cycle, which articulates the univer-
sality of the concept of shimmering. Because of its unique structure,
mode 7 can also be used to represent Godly and heavenly ideas.

Another reason why Messiaen presents shimmering by mode 7 is that both the universal and the person who is observing the universal are present. In so doing, he ascribes two different meanings to mode 7, one universal and one human.

Thème d'accords includes both the octatonic scale and perfect fifths. The stanza "the powerful breaths sounding immense trombones" are presented by the rhythmic canons. The breaths are all made up of tritones. The breaths, the canons, start right after each other and continue in the same way until the trombones are brought in. The trombones are presented in the bass by octatonic scales which are against the perfect fifths of the breaths. Fire, a universal concept, is articulated by perfect fifths, whereas the servants are articulated by the octatonic collections.

Section B is related to the stanza "then the song of birds, drinking azure." In this section, mode 7—which is asymmetical in structure—represents earthly things. However, there are no longer perfect fifth cycles appearing in the music. At this point, Messiaen no longer uses perfect fifths because these would be representative of the universal.

The coda stanza "Angels are amazed. God joins them with the human race" is primarily made up of octatonic collections and represents the amazement of the angels as well as the fact that God joins humanity.

In *Je Dors, Mais Mon Cœur Veille*, Messiaen added a sixteenth-note to one of the values in almost every measure of the opening section in order to ruin the systematic division which represents the human perception of time. These kinds of rhythmic changes are extremely important in the delineation of the musical form.

While using an extra-musical source as a program for musical composition is nothing new, the manner in which Messiaen uses different pitch collections and special rhythms to represent unique concepts is highly sophisticated. The complex pitch relations generated by the simultaneous use of different pitch collections and their derivatives articulate several things. They not only reflect the literal meaning of the title (word painting) but also articulate a progression and amalgamation of literal and abstract concepts which follow one another, simultaneously generating both a literal history and the musical progression and formal structure of the piece.

Bibliography

Bruhn, Siglind. *Images and Ideas in Modern French Piano Music: The Extra-Musical Subtext in Piano Works by Ravel, Debussy, and Messiaen.* Stuyvesant, NY: Pendragon, 1997.

———. *Messiaen's Contemplations of Covenant and Incarnation: Musical Symbols of Faith in the Two Great Piano Cycles of the 1940s.* Hillsdale, NY: Pendragon, 2007.

———. *Messiaen's Explorations of Love and Death: Musico-Poetic Signification in the "Tristan Trilogy" and Three Related Song Cycles.* Hillsdale, NY: Pendragon, 2008.

———. *Messiaen's Language of Mystical Love.* New York: Routledge, 2012.

Bullinger, E. W. *Number in Scripture: Its Supernatural Design and Spiritual Significance.* Grand Rapids, MI: Kregel, 1988.

Burger, Cole Philip. "Olivier Messiaen's Vingt Regards sur l'enfant-Jesus: Analytical, Religious, and Literary Considerations." DMA diss., University of Texas at Austin, 2009. https://repositories.lib.utexas.edu/bitstream/handle/2152/7541/burgerc67661.pdf?sequence=2&isAllowed=y.

Griffiths, Paul. *Olivier Messiaen and the Music of Time.* Ithaca, NY: Cornell University Press, 1985.

Johnson, Robert Sherlaw. *Messiaen.* Berkeley, CA: University of California Press, 1980.

Kavanaugh, Patrick. *Spiritual Lives of the Great Composers.* Grand Rapids, MI: Zondervan, 1996.

Messiaen, Olivier. *The Technique of My Musical Language: Text with Musical Examples.* Translated by J. Satterfield. Paris: Alphonse Leduc, 2007.

Van Der Walt, Salomé. "Rhythmic Techniques in a Selection of Olivier Messiaen's Piano Works." Master's thesis, University of Pretoria, 2007. http://www.repository.up.ac.za/bitstream/handle/2263/25190/dissertation.pdf?sequence=1&isAllowed=y.

Voglar, Inés. "Fear No Music: Exploring and Performing Great Music of the Twentieth and Twenty-first Centuries, and Promoting Education and Advancement of Young Composers." https://unbornwordoftheday.files.wordpress.com/2011/06/program-notes-for-twenty-glances-on-the-infant-jesusvingt-regards-sur-l_enfant-jc3a9sus1.pdf.

www.ingramcontent.com/pod-product-compliance
Lightning Source LLC
LaVergne TN
LVHW051711080426
835511LV00017B/2861